MW00778133

You Have to Fucking Eat

by Adam Mansbach

illustrated by Owen Brozman

All rights reserved. No part of this book may be reproduced, stored in a retrieval system, or transmitted in any form, by any means, including mechanical, electronic, photocopying, recording, or otherwise, without the prior written consent of the publisher.

Published by Akashic Books
Words ©2014 Adam Mansbach
Illustrations ©2014 Owen Brozman

ISBN: 978-1-61775-378-7
Third printing

Printed in China

Akashic Books
Instagram, Twitter, Facebook:
AkashicBooks
info@akashicbooks.com
www.akashicbooks.com

Adam Mansbach is the author of the #1 international best seller *Go the Fuck to Sleep* and *Fuck, Now There Are Two of You*, the third book in the series. He is an award-winning novelist, humorist, and screenwriter whose works include the novels *Rage Is Back, Angry Black White Boy,* and *The End of the Jews*, the screenplay for the Netflix original film *Barry*, and *A Field Guide to the Jewish People*, coauthored with Dave Barry and Alan Zweibel.

www.AdamMansbach.com

Owen Brozman is the illustrator of *Fuck, Now There Are Two of You* by Adam Mansbach. His other work includes comics, advertisements, murals, album covers, magazines, and more. He illustrated the cookbook *Kindness & Salt* and the graphic novel *Nature of the Beast*, and has worked with Scholastic, *Entertainment Weekly, Time Out New York*, and numerous other clients. He lives with his family in Brooklyn, New York.

www.OwenBrozman.com

For Vivien and Olivia

The sunrise is golden and lovely,
The birds chirp and twitter and tweet,
You woke me and asked for some breakfast,
So why the fuck won't you eat?

The bunnies are munching on carrots,
The lambs nibble grasses and bleat.
I know you're too hungry to reason with but
You have to fucking eat.

Your cute little tummy is rumbling
And pancakes are your favorite treat.
I'm kind of surprised that you suddenly hate them.
That's bullshit. Stop lying and eat.

The giraffes pluck the tender young leaves up,
The mice snack on seeds and on wheat.
No, sweetheart, I can't make spaghetti,
The fucking meal's served. Time to eat.

If we were both pandas I'd know what to feed you,
But seafood is scary, we're leery of meat.
Half the food at the market is probably toxic,
But fuck it, you still have to eat.

You're not finished, and no, you can't go to school
In pajamas, a hat, and bare feet.
Whatever, put shoes on and bring me your plate,
My whole diet's the shit you won't eat.

The sloth and the lemur, the chipmunk and cheetah,
The slow and the sleek and the fleet
Share one thing, my love: they make less of a mess
Than you fucking do when they eat.

You know who loves dinner? The duck-billed platypus.
But I know I'm facing defeat.
This spoon-feeding shit makes me wonder
Why the fuck we weaned you from the teat.

I hope you know it's super-special
To go to a restau— Hey, back in your seat.
You shitting me? This whole menu's crap to you
But a roll on the floor—*that* you'll eat?

Yum, this looks great. Five big bites, my darling.
Fine. Three, but don't try to cheat.
A lot of kids don't get asparagus,
Show some fucking respect for them. Eat.

Oh, now you're hungry? Tough shit, kitchen's closed.
Have some warm milk. For me a scotch, neat.
Pancakes? Yeah, right. It's bedtime, child,
It's too goddamn late now to eat.

Okay. One pancake and that's it,
You're exhausting and I'm fucking beat.
And tomorrow we've got to rise early as roosters
To fight more about what to eat.

I'm pretty sure that you're malnourished
And scurvied. My failure's complete.
But on the bright side, maybe this is the night
You'll go the fuck to sleep.

The End

Go the Fuck to Sleep

by Adam Mansbach

illustrated by Ricardo Cortés

All rights reserved. No part of this book may be reproduced, stored in a retrieval system, or transmitted in any form, by any means, including mechanical, electronic, photocopying, recording, or otherwise, without the prior written consent of the publisher.

Published by Akashic Books
Words ©2011 Adam Mansbach
Illustrations ©2011 Ricardo Cortés

ISBN-13: 978-1-61775-025-0
Twenty-sixth printing
Printed in China

Akashic Books
Brooklyn, New York
Instagram: AkashicBooks
Twitter: AkashicBooks
Facebook: AkashicBooks
E-mail: info@akashicbooks.com
Website: www.akashicbooks.com

Adam Mansbach is the author of *Fuck, Now There Are Two of You* and *You Have to Fucking Eat*, the international best-selling follow-ups to *Go the Fuck to Sleep*. He is an award-winning novelist and screenwriter whose books include *Rage Is Back*, *The End of the Jews*, and *Angry Black White Boy*. His work has appeared in the *New Yorker*, the *New York Times Book Review, Esquire,* the *Believer,* and on National Public Radio's *The Moth, This American Life*, and *All Things Considered*. His daughters are twelve, three, and one.

www.AdamMansbach.com

Ricardo Cortés illustrated *Go the Fuck to Sleep* and its companions *Go de Rass to Sleep* and *Seriously, Just Go to Sleep*. He also illustrated *Party: A Mystery* by Jamaica Kincaid, and is the author/illustrator of *It's Just a Plant: A Children's Story about Marijuana; A Secret History of Coffee, Coca & Cola;* and *Sea Creatures from the Sky*.

www.Rmcortes.com

for Vivien, without whom none of this would be possible

The cats nestle close to their kittens,
The lambs have lain down with the sheep.
You're cozy and warm in your bed, my dear.
 Please go the fuck to sleep.

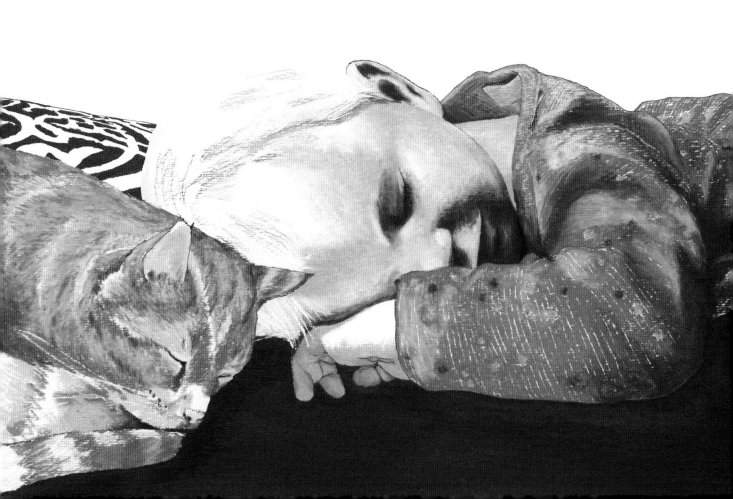

The windows are dark in the town, child.
The whales huddle down in the deep.
I'll read you one very last book if you swear
You'll go the fuck to sleep.

The eagles who soar through the sky are at rest
And the creatures who crawl, run, and creep.
I know you're not thirsty. That's bullshit. Stop lying.
Lie the fuck down, my darling, and sleep.

The wind whispers soft through the grass, hon.
The field mice, they make not a peep.
It's been thirty-eight minutes already.
Jesus Christ, what the fuck? Go to sleep.

All the kids from day care are in dreamland.
The froggie has made his last leap.
Hell no, you can't go to the bathroom.
You know where you can go? The fuck to sleep.

The owls fly forth from the treetops.
Through the air, they soar and they sweep.
A hot crimson rage fills my heart, love.
For real, shut the fuck up and sleep.

The cubs and the lions are snoring,
Wrapped in a big snuggly heap.
How come you can do all this other great shit
But you can't lie the fuck down and sleep?

The seeds slumber beneath the earth now
And the crops that the farmers will reap.
No more questions. This interview's over.
I've got two words for you, kid: fucking sleep.

The tiger reclines in the simmering jungle.
The sparrow has silenced her cheep.
Fuck your stuffed bear, I'm not getting you shit.
Close your eyes. Cut the crap. Sleep.

The flowers doze low in the meadows
And high on the mountains so steep.
My life is a failure, I'm a shitty-ass parent.
Stop fucking with me, please, and sleep.

The giant pangolins of Madagascar are snoozing
As I lie here and openly weep.
Sure, fine, whatever, I'll bring you some milk.
Who the fuck cares? You're not gonna sleep.

This room is all I can remember,
The furniture crappy and cheap.
You win. You escape. You run down the hall.
As I nod the fuck off, and sleep.

Bleary and dazed I awaken
To find your eyes shut, so I keep
My fingers crossed tight as I tiptoe away
And pray that you're fucking asleep.

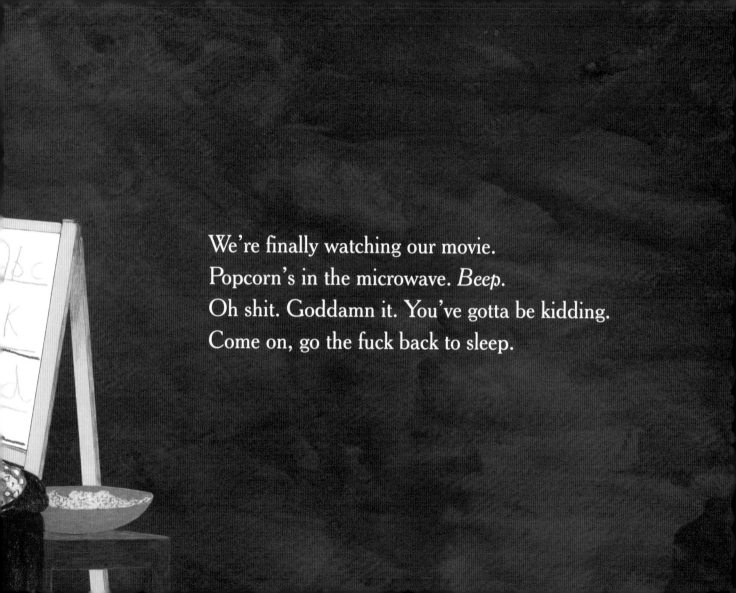

We're finally watching our movie.
Popcorn's in the microwave. *Beep.*
Oh shit. Goddamn it. You've gotta be kidding.
Come on, go the fuck back to sleep.

The End

Fuck, Now There Are Two of You

by Adam Mansbach

illustrated by Owen Brozman

All rights reserved. No part of this book may be
reproduced, stored in a retrieval system, or transmitted
in any form, by any means, including mechanical,
electronic, photocopying, recording, or otherwise,
without the prior written consent of the publisher.

Published by Akashic Books
Words ©2019 Adam Mansbach
Illustrations ©2019 Owen Brozman

ISBN-13: 978-1-61775-760-0
First printing
Printed in Malaysia

Akashic Books
Brooklyn, New York, USA
Ballydehob, Co. Cork, Ireland
Twitter: @AkashicBooks
Facebook: AkashicBooks
E-mail: info@akashicbooks.com
Website: www.akashicbooks.com

Adam Mansbach is an award-winning novelist, humorist, and screenwriter whose works include the novels *Rage
Is Back, Angry Black White Boy,* and *The End of the Jews,* the
screenplay for the Netflix Original film *Barry,* and, most
recently—with Dave Barry and Alan Zweibel—*A Field
Guide to the Jewish People.* He actually has *three* children,
two of whom are under two years old. Please send help.

www.AdamMansbach.com

Owen Brozman is an illustrator whose work includes
comics, advertisements, murals, album covers, magazines,
and more. He illustrated the cookbook *Kindness & Salt,*
the graphic novel *Nature of the Beast,* and the previous en-
try in this series, *You Have to Fucking Eat.* He has worked
with Scholastic, *Entertainment Weekly, Time Out New York,*
and numerous other clients. He lives with his family in
Brooklyn, New York.

www.OwenBrozman.com

For Zanthe and Asa, and Olivia

I have wonderful news for you, darling.
A little brother or sister is coming—what fun!
As for me, my life's pretty much fucked now
Because two's a million more kids than one.

The baby is growing inside Mama's tummy.
Put your hand there—you might feel a kick!
Soon you won't be the focus of all our attention.
Chances are, that will make you a dick.

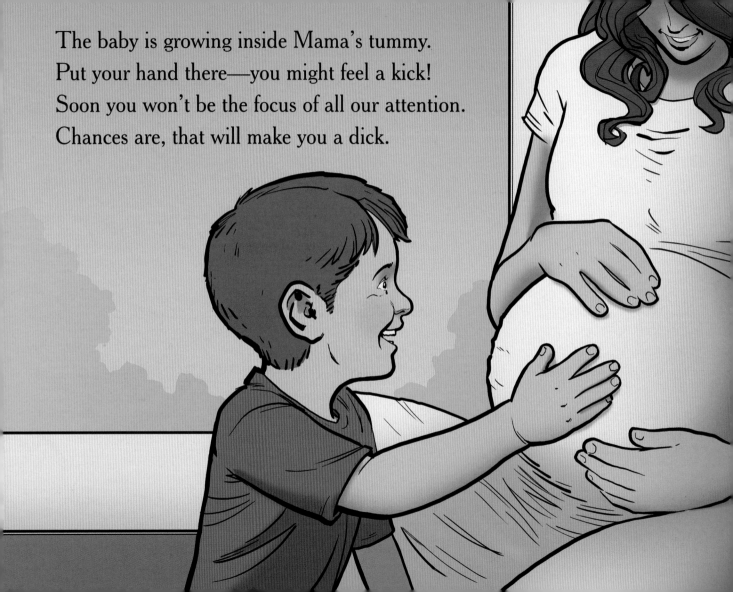

I never knew love before you came
And I swore that one kid would be it, so
This is a big change for us all, hon.
Our life is one gigantic shit show.

Once there were pockets of quiet
When Mama and Papa could do a few
Grown-up-type things, but not anymore.
Fuck! Now there are two of you.

No, I can't play right now, kiddo.
The babe spent the whole night awake.
I know you feel sad and neglected
But cut me some slack, for fuck's sake.

Wow, so now you're an infant again?
You're watching the baby and following suit?
I don't know how to break this to you, love,
But that shit is not fucking cute.

Looking back, with just you it was easy
To do stuff without a big uproar.
Now the simplest outing's a grueling ordeal.
What the fuck did we sign ourselves up for?

You're so loving and sweet with the baby,
Snuggled in bed, side by side.
It makes me wish I could forget your attempts
At motherfucking fratricide.

Someday you'll entertain one another
While we chill and catch up on our reading.
But for years—fucking years!—there will not be a time
No one's shitting or crying or peeing.

I don't love you any less now, my dear.
Love's not a pie; we don't have to divide it.
I'm just so frazzled I hate everybody
And I'm too fucking tired to hide it.

Sorry, sweetheart, we can't go to the playground.
The baby's so big now—it's tricky to manage her!
And I'll be damned if I let myself be
Outnumbered like some fucking amateur.

The floor and all four walls are covered
In vegetables, pasta, and fruit.
I can vaguely remember when meals did not
require fucking hazmat suits.

Sometimes when you both are sleeping,
We watch you, secure in the knowledge
That one day this madness will come to an end
And you'll both go the fuck off to college.

At two in the morning it hits me.
My heart thumps a-rat-a-tat-tat.
If you two are going to college
How the fuck are we paying for that?

The End